My Trip to the Zoo

An Interactive Book about Me

Developed by K.A. Bye

Illustrated by Earl W. Ridgell, Jr.

BOYS TOWN Press

Boys Town, Nebraska

Dedication

*The **Interactive Book about Me** series is dedicated to my husband, children, and grandchildren – each a continuous source of inspiration for my own adventures in writing.*

My Trip to the Zoo

ISBN-13 978-1-934490-00-6
ISBN-10 1-934490-00-8

Cover and interior design by Anne Hughes
Edited by Barbara Lonnborg
Production by Russ Cappello

Printed in China
10 9 8 7 6 5 4 3 2 1

Published by **Boys Town Press**
14100 Crawford St.
Boys Town, NE 68010

BOYS TOWN
Saving Children Healing Families

For a Boys Town Press catalog, call 1-800-282-6657
or visit our Web site: www.boystownpress.org

I think going to the zoo is a lot of fun.
There is so much to see and do.

I am going to tell you about
my trip to the zoo.

My name is

______________________________.

This is me ______________________________

______________________________ at the zoo.

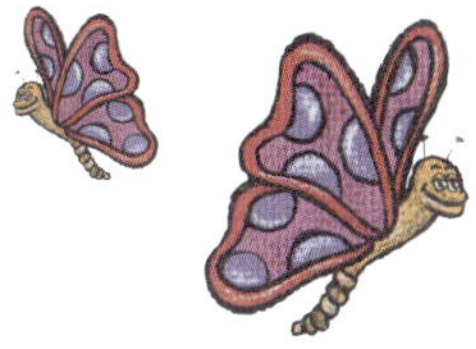

I like going to the zoo with __________

____

______________________________.

Animals are everywhere
at the zoo.

The animals are in all shapes and sizes.

Some of the animals I saw at the zoo are ______________________

____

____.

Some animals at the zoo
are shorter than me.

_________________________ is a very short animal.

It has short _________________________

and _________________________.

Some animals at the zoo
are taller than me.

_______________ is a very tall animal.

It has _______________

and _______________.

Some animals are smaller than me.

See how small the ______________________________ is.

It ____

____.

Some animals are bigger than me.

________________________ is the biggest animal

I saw at the zoo. It ________________________

____________________________________.

Many different kinds of animals live at the zoo.

Birds are animals at the zoo.

This is my favorite bird.

It is called a ________________________________.

It has a ________________ and ________________.

Other kinds of animals live at the zoo.

Fish are there, too.

This fish is my favorite fish.

It is called a ______________________________.

It has a ______________________________

and ______________________________.

Some animals at the zoo are noisy.

I think the noisiest animal at the zoo

is the ____________________________.

Some animals at the zoo are quiet.

I think the quietest animal at the zoo

is the ______________________________.

Some animals at the zoo look friendly.

I think the friendliest looking animal at the zoo

is the ______________________________.

Some animals at the zoo look scary.

I think the scariest looking animal at the zoo

is the ______________________________.

There is so much to see and do at the zoo.

Besides looking at all of the animals,

I like to ______________________________

____.

Of everything I saw at the zoo,

I like ________________________________

________________________________ best.

I like it because ____

____

____.

I have so much fun at the zoo.

I____________________________________

_____________________________________.

I hope I get to go again soon!

- Mother of 3-year-old

- 6-year-old

- 6-year-old

- Mother and 5 -year-old

How to Use This Interactive Book about Me

Parents/Grandparents/Caregivers

There are many ways to use this interactive book to stimulate your child's creativity and interest in reading and writing. Older children will enjoy completing the sentences, choosing photographs or drawing pictures to create the book on their own. Very young children may require help with printing and pasting. However, be sure to ask for their input. Ask your child questions before deciding on how to complete the sentences, such as: "Which was the noisiest animal you heard at the zoo? Which one was the tallest? What part of visiting the zoo did you like best and why?" Let the child choose the photographs to use or draw pictures to accompany the text. The shared activity of working and having fun together is one of the great benefits this book can bring you and your child.

How simple or elaborate this book becomes is entirely up to you and your child. Young children may become excited to see and read the entire book with you, so it's possible to finish the book by just completing the text and gluing a photo on each page. If you or your child enjoys the hobby of scrapbooking, you can work on the book in slower stages and add colorful borders, cutouts, or stickers. The printed illustrations and borders are there to enliven the pages for children, but don't be afraid to cover them up with extra photos or decorations of your own choosing. You can also encourage children to add more text to the pages if they wish. To the left are examples of pages from ***My Trip to the Zoo*** completed by parents and children.

Many children return to these interactive books over and over again – to read or "tell" the stories to themselves and to share with friends, grandparents, and yes, even the family dog! And, because the book centers on words and pictures from the child's own experiences, it may stimulate greater interest in reading than traditional storybooks do for children with learning, developmental or behavioral challenges. Reading aloud to and with children is the most important activity you can do to assure their success in reading. However you choose to use this book, enjoy the journey it allows you to share with your child!

***NOTE:* We recommend that children use crayons or colored pencils when working on this book. If using markers, please test for bleed-through before proceeding.**

Educators

One of the keys to learning to read is motivation. This interactive book, in which the child provides the text and the important images, creates that motivation. It will engage your students in the development of reading skills and vocabulary through individual life experiences. The book's basic text utilizes Dolch Sight Words in establishing sentence starters for children. (Flesch-Kincaid Readability Level for supplied text is 1.8.) Additional vocabulary specific to content is introduced with words added by students and supported by images (photos or drawings) supplied by them.

My Trip to the Zoo helps children:

- Identify groups of animals (e.g., birds, fish)
- Understand common language of measurement (e.g., short, tall)
- Use terms of comparison (e.g., small, big, noisy, quiet)
- Understand the concept of print
- Understand that illustrations and pictures convey meaning
- Use descriptive language
- Use new vocabulary to describe experiences
- Read familiar stories aloud

– 5-year-old

Books in the ***Interactive Book about Me*** series are designed to help all beginning readers and writers, including English language learners and students identified for Title I or special education programs. The words and images are "owned" by them because they come from the students' own lives. The books require them to think critically, recall and reflect on their experiences, and then recount them in writing – all helpful in developing language skills.

One great way to utilize these books in your classes is to have your students begin or complete one in preparation for a parents' open house or parent-teacher conference. They allow you to demonstrate the students' progress in reading and writing with the end product being a book that parents can take home for shared reading aloud with their child.

If you would like to use any book from the ***Interactive Book about Me*** series in your classroom, you may contact the Boys Town Press at 1-800-282-6657 for information about quantity discounts.

Interactive Children's Books from Boys Town Press

ISBN-13 978-1-934490-00-6; ISBN-10 1-934490-00-8

My Trip to the Zoo

An Interactive Book about Me

By K.A. Bye, M.S., illustrated by Earl W. Ridgell, Jr.

Your child creates a book about his or her trip to the zoo by describing many of the animals encountered there – the short, tall, big, small, noisy, quiet, friendly and scary ones. Other favorite zoo activities are included.

For ages 2-8; $13.95; 30 pgs. hardcover; color illus.; 10" x 8"

ISBN-13 978-1-934490-03-7; ISBN-10 1-934490-03-2

I Like Holidays!

An Interactive Book about Me

By K.A. Bye, M.S., illustrated by Earl W. Ridgell, Jr.

Your child will record your family's cherished traditions connected to a favorite holiday. Whatever the holiday, he or she will describe the people you share it with and the colors, decorations, clothing, food, and stories you use to celebrate it.

For ages 2-8; $13.95; 30 pgs. hardcover; color illus.; 10" x 8"

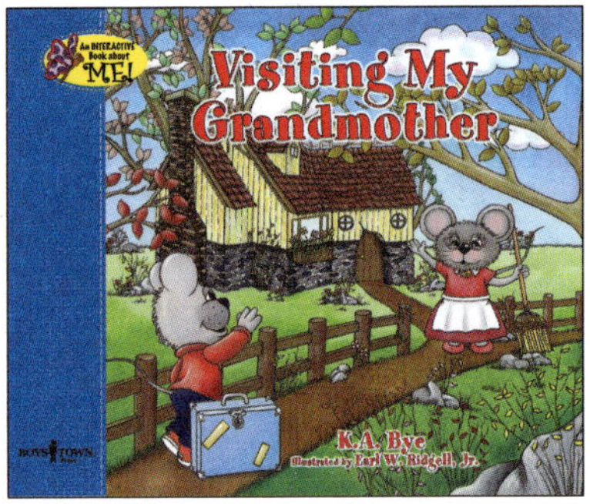

ISBN-13 978-1-934490-01-3; ISBN-10 1-934490-01-6

Visiting My Grandmother

An Interactive Book about Me

By K.A. Bye, M.S., illustrated by Earl W. Ridgell, Jr.

This book helps your child write about a visit to Grandmother – what she looks like, where she lives, how they play and what they do and eat together. Your child will also describe their feelings for each other.

For ages 2-8; $13.95; 30 pgs. hardcover; color illus.; 10" x 8"

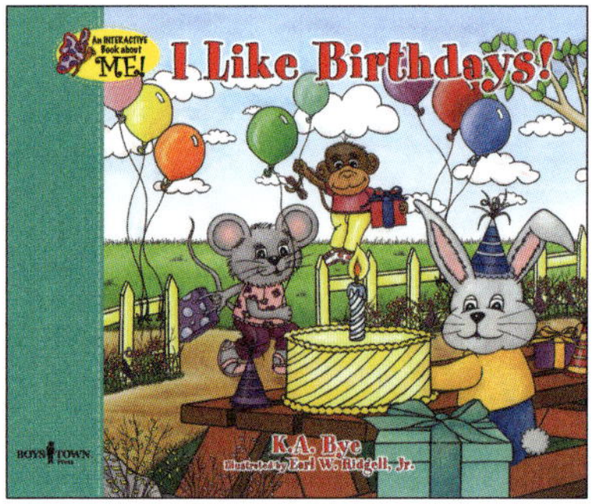

ISBN-13 978-1-934490-02-0; ISBN-10 1-934490-02-4

I Like Birthdays!

An Interactive Book about Me

By K.A. Bye, M.S., illustrated by Earl W. Ridgell, Jr.

The number of candles on the cake, the friends and family there, the special food and clothing, the favorite presents – your child will share through this book all the wonderful people and events that make a birthday such a happy occasion!

For ages 2-8; $13.95; 30 pgs. hardcover; color illus.; 10" x 8"

Boys Town Press
14100 Crawford St., Boys Town, NE 68010
Toll-free 1-800-282-6657
Fax 1-402-498-1310
E-mail: btpress@boystown.org
Web site: www.boystownpress.org